LOOK AND SEE 2

ACTIVITY BOOK

NATIONAL GEOGRAPHIC
LEARNING

Australia • Brazil • Mexico • Singapore • United Kingdom • United States

1 TR: 0.1 Listen, point, and say.

1 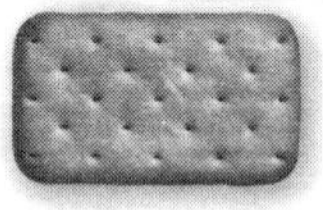

2 

3 

4 

5 

6 

7 

8 

9 

10 

2 TR: 0.2 Listen and chant.

3 TR: 0.3 Listen, point, and say.

A 

ALLIGATOR

E 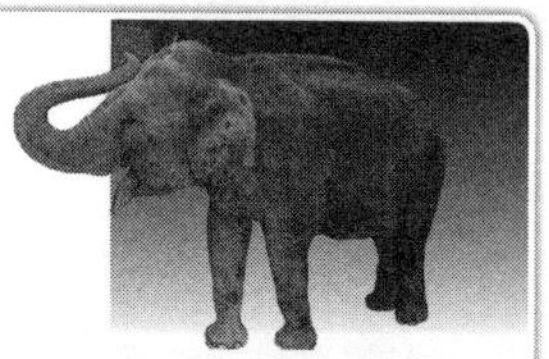

ELEPHANT

I 

IGUANA

O 

OCTOPUS

U 

UMBRELLABIRD

1 Draw you. Say.

UNIT

1 AT SCHOOL

1 TR: 1.1 Listen and circle.

2 Point and say.

NEW WORDS: *blocks, friend, teacher; glue, markers, paper, scissors*

1 Draw your family and friends. Then point and say.

1 TR: 1.2 Circle. Then listen, sing, and point.

2 Look and circle ✔ or ✘.

VALUE **BE NEAT IN THE CLASSROOM.**

1 ✔ ✘

2 ✔ ✘

3 ✔ ✘

1 TR: 1.3 Listen and say.

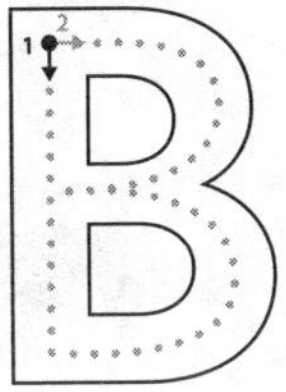

BEAVER

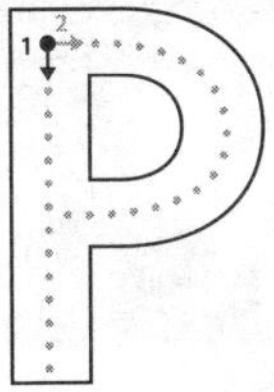

PANDA

2 Trace.

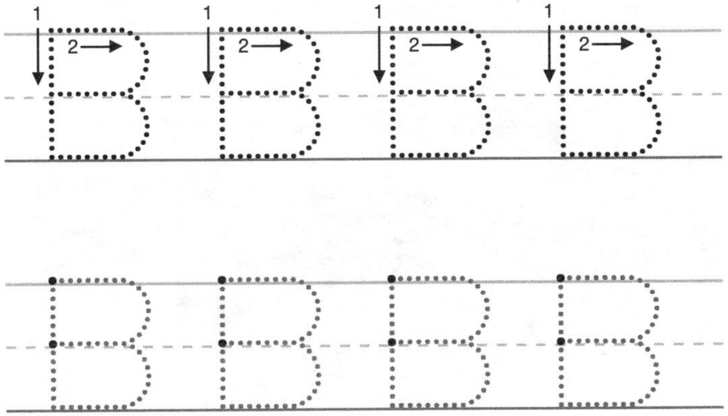

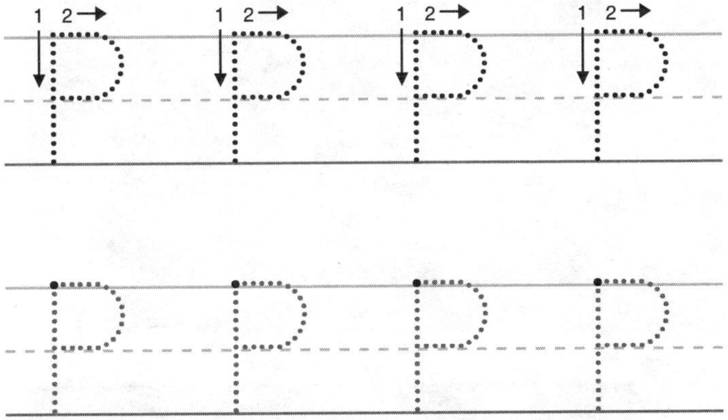

1 TR: 1.4 Listen and match.

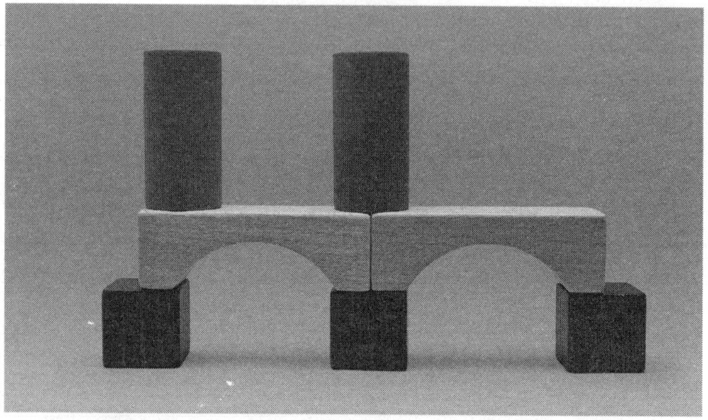

 VIDEO: SC: 2 *(optional)* **Content Words:** *big, bridge, house, small, tower*

1 **TR: 1.5** Listen and point. Then say and color.

REVIEW: NEW WORDS: *blocks, friend, teacher; glue, markers, paper, scissors*
STRUCTURE: *Who's this? He's my grandpa. She's my friend.*

UNIT

2 ARE YOU HAPPY?

1 TR: 2.1 Listen. Circle ✔ or ✘.

1 (✔) ✘

2 ✔ ✘

3 ✔ ✘

4 ✔ ✘

5 ✔ ✘

6 ✔ ✘

7 ✔ ✘

2 Point and say.

 NEW WORDS: *angry, excited, happy, hungry, sad, sleepy, thirsty*

1 Draw you. Then point and say.

1 TR: 2.2 Listen and circle. Then listen, sing, and point.

2 Look and circle ✔ or ✘.

VALUE **GET A GOOD NIGHT'S SLEEP.**

1 ✔ ✘

2 ✔ ✘

3 ✔ ✘

1 TR: 2.3 Listen and say.

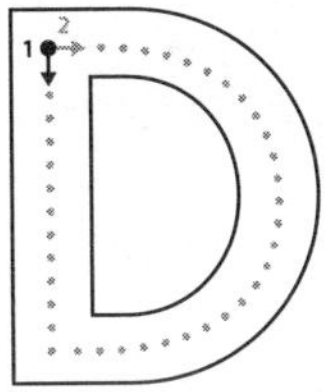

DUCK

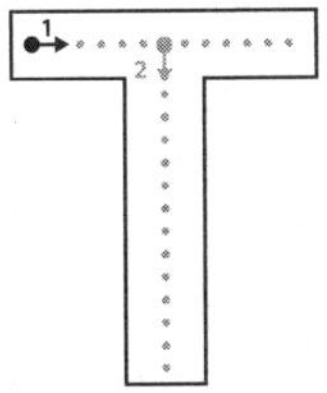

TIGER

2 Trace.

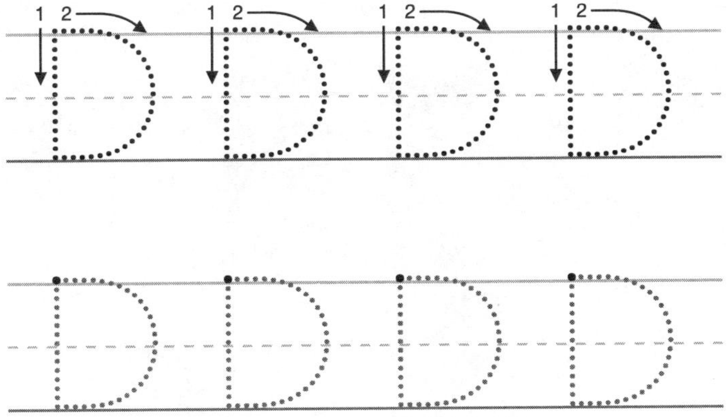

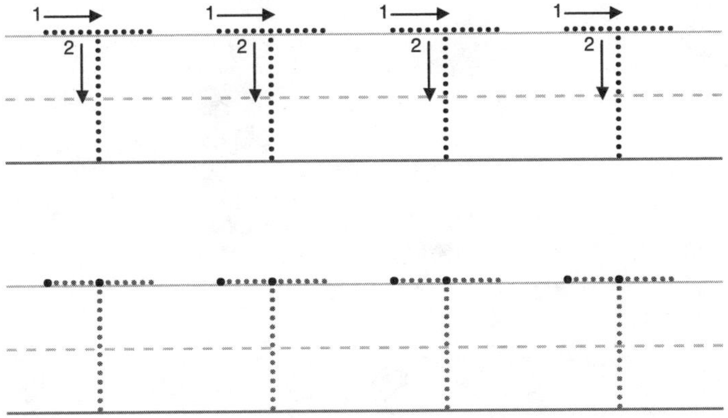

1 TR: 2.4 Listen and match. Then color your favorite.

1 2 3 4

 VIDEO: SC: 4 *(optional)* **Content Words:** *loud, music, quiet*

1 Play and say.

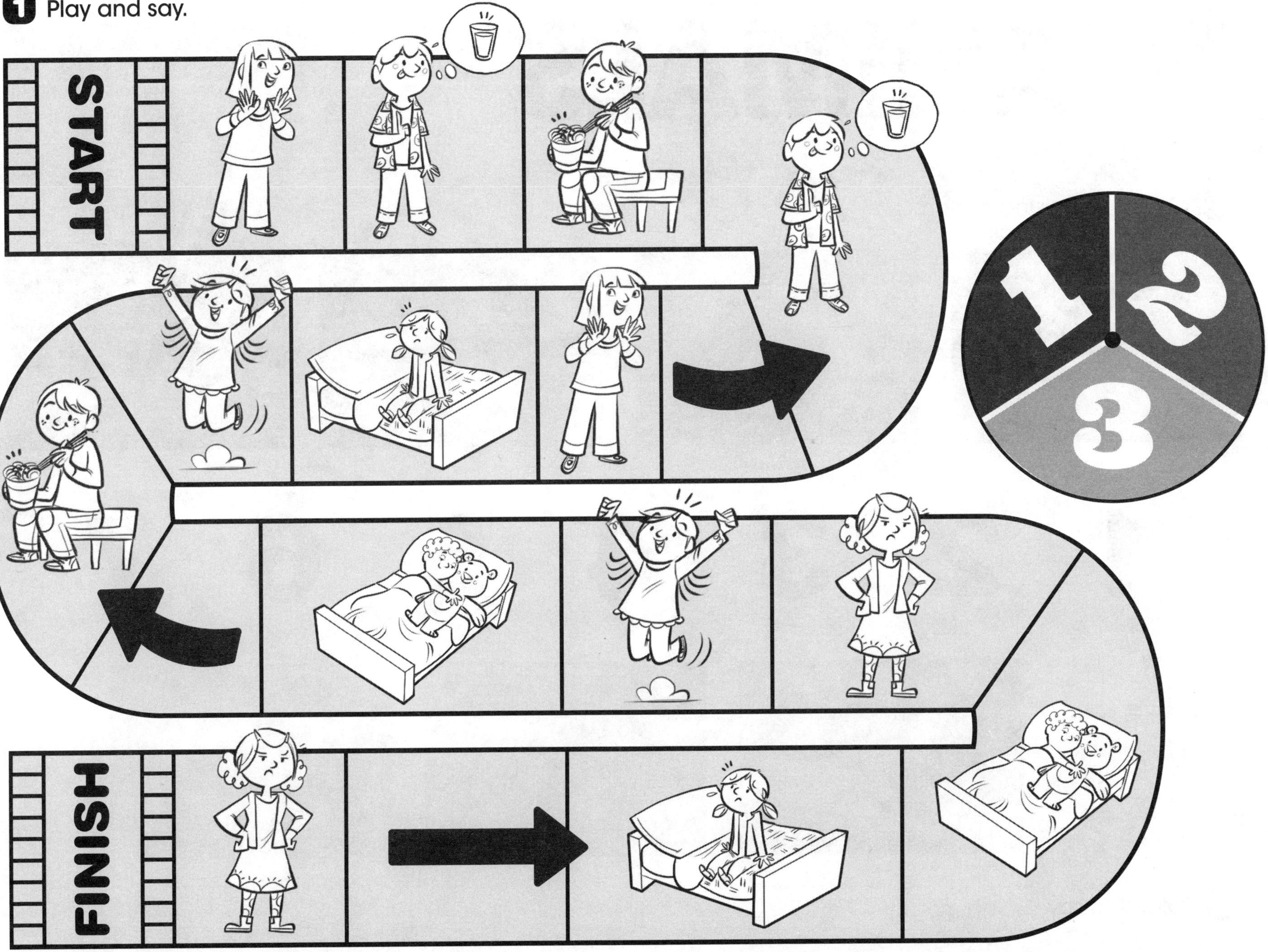

REVIEW: NEW WORDS: *angry, excited, happy, hungry, sad, sleepy, thirsty*
STRUCTURE: *Are you happy? Yes, I am. Are you sad? No, I'm not.*

UNIT 3 ANIMALS

1 TR: 3.1 Listen and match.

1 2 3 4 5 6 7

2 Point and say.

 NEW WORDS: *bat, bear, duck, fox, owl, rabbit, snake*

1 Match. Then ask and answer.

1 TR: 3.2 Listen and color. Then listen, sing, and point.

2 Look and circle ✔ or ✘.

VALUE **BE CURIOUS ABOUT ANIMALS.**

1 ✔ ✘

2 ✔ ✘

3 ✔ ✘

1 TR: 3.3 Listen and say.

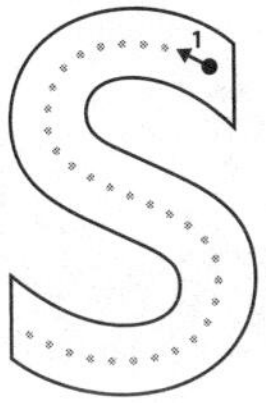

SEAL

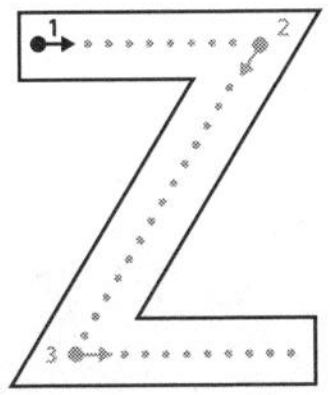

ZEBRA

2 Trace.

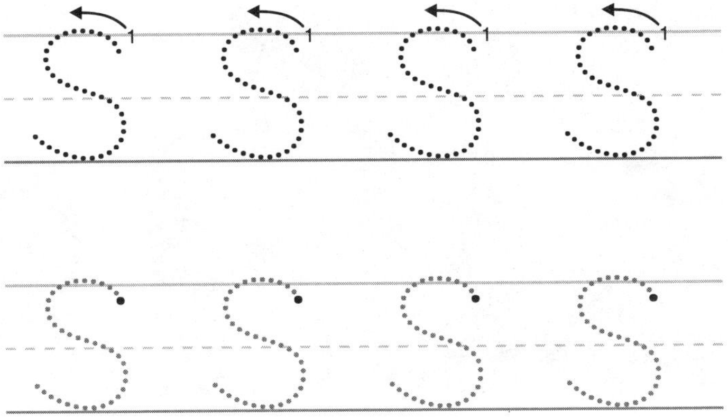

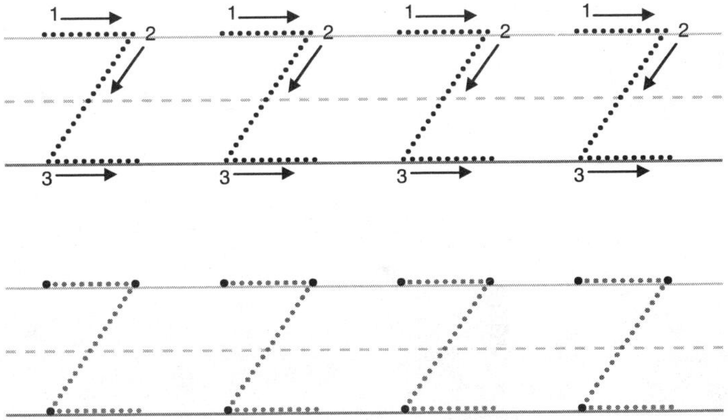

1 TR: 3.4 Look and match. Then listen and check.

1 Find and color. Then ask and answer.

REVIEW: NEW WORDS: *bat, bear, duck, fox, owl, rabbit, snake*
STRUCTURE: *What is it? It's an owl. What are they? They're bears.*

UNIT

4 GET DRESSED

1 TR: 4.1 Listen and point.

2 Point and say.

NEW WORDS: *boots, coat, dress, pants, scarf, skirt, sweater*

1 Draw and color. Then match and say.

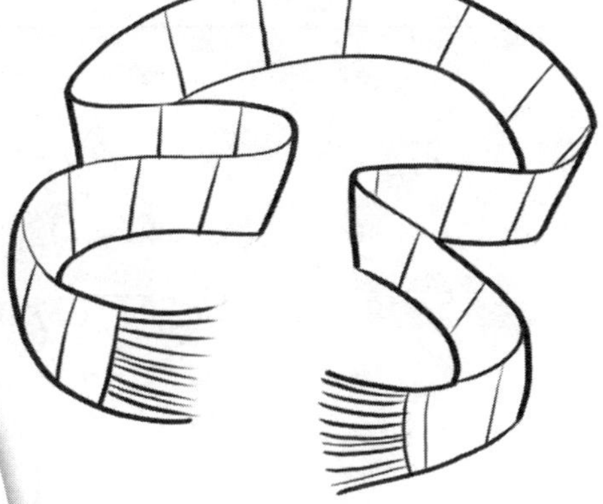

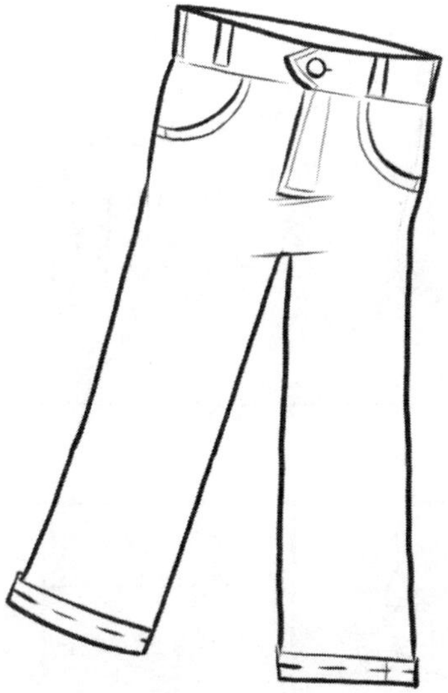

STRUCTURE: *This is my sweater. These are my pants.*

1 TR: 4.2 Listen, sing, and point.

2 Look and circle ✔ or ✘.

VALUE **DRESS FOR THE WEATHER.**

1 ✔ ✘

2 ✔ ✘

3 ✔ ✘

1 TR: 4.3 Listen and say.

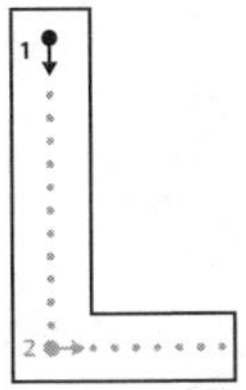

LION

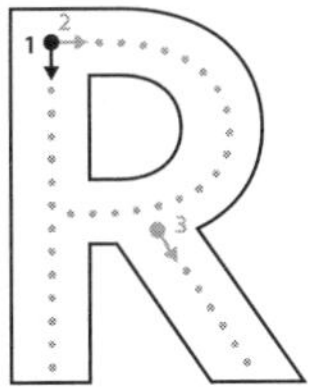

REINDEER

2 Trace.

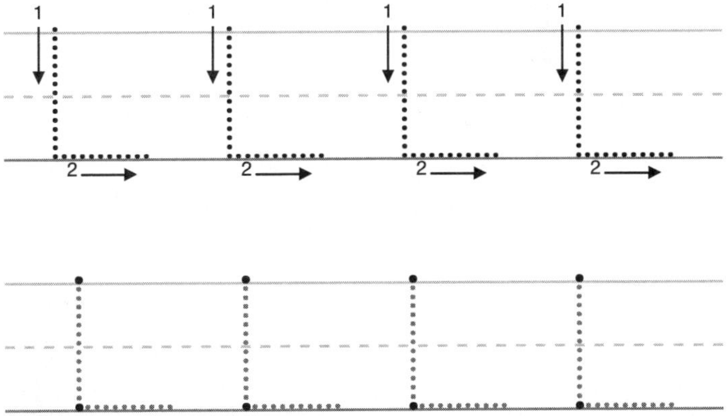

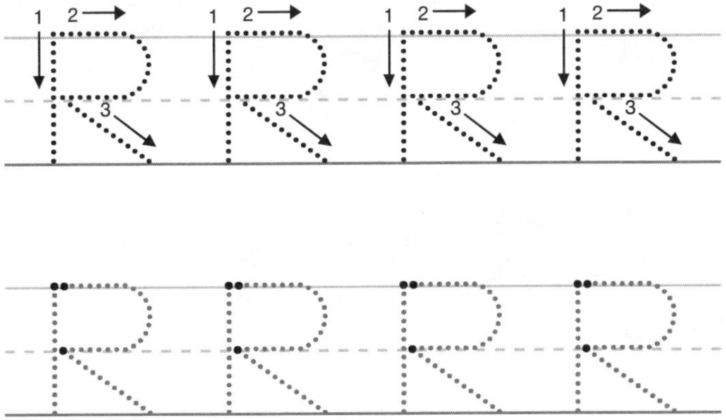

1 TR: 4.4 Listen and match.

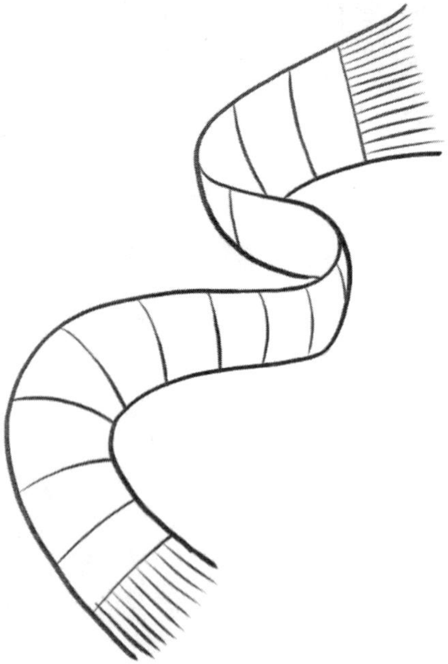

 VIDEO: SC: 8 *(optional)* **Content Words:** *cotton, plant, silk, worm*

1 Color. Play and say.

UNIT

5 I CAN JUMP!

1 TR: 5.1 Listen. Circle ✔ or ✘.

1 ✔ ✘

2 ✔ ✘

3 ✔ ✘

4 ✔ ✘

5 ✔ ✘

6 ✔ ✘

7 ✔ ✘

2 Point and say.

 NEW WORDS: *crawl, dance, hop, jump, run, turn around, walk*

1 Do and say.

1 TR: 5.2 Listen and point. Then sing and do.

2 Look and circle ✔ or ✘.

VALUE **PLAY OUTSIDE.**

1 ✔ ✘

2 ✔ ✘

3 ✔ ✘

1 TR: 5.3 Listen and say.

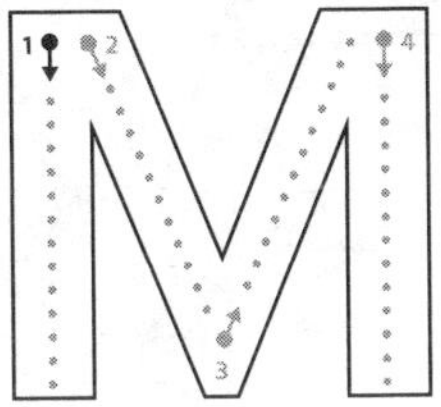

MONKEY

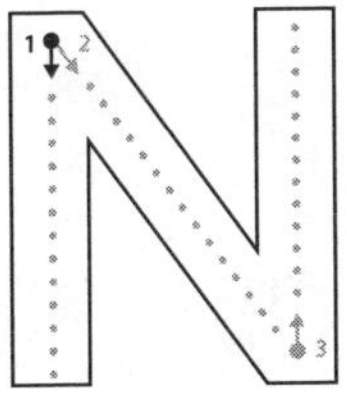

NUMBAT

2 Trace.

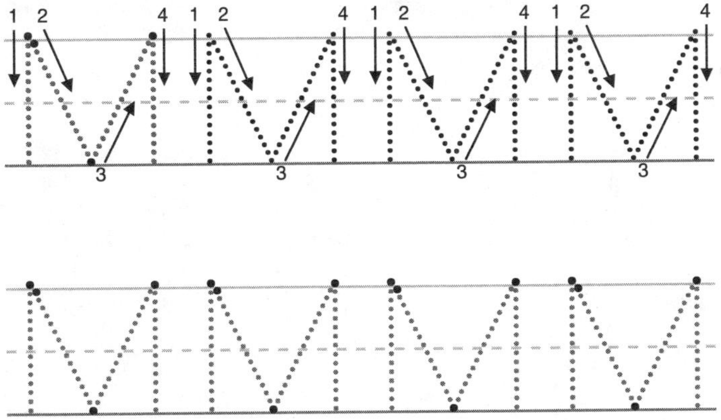

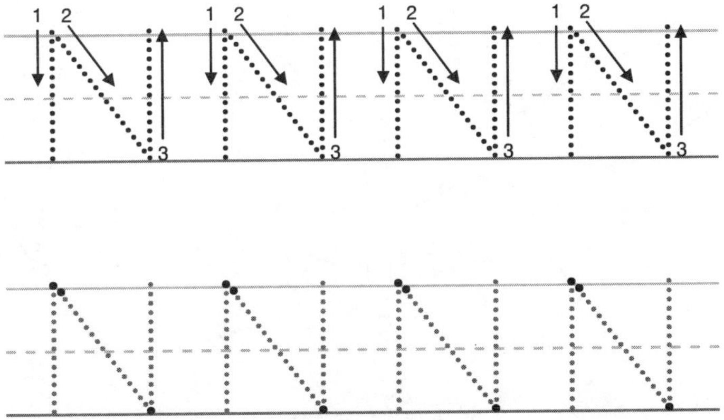

1 TR: 5.4 Listen and color.

1 What can you do? Color, say, and do.

REVIEW: NEW WORDS: *crawl, dance, hop, jump, run, turn around, walk*
STRUCTURE: *I can hop.*

UNIT 6 FACES

1 TR: 6.1 Listen and point.

2 TR: 6.2 Listen and draw.

1

2

3

 NEW WORDS: *ears, eyes, face, hair, mouth, nose; long, short*

1 TR: 6.3 Listen. Then draw and color. Say.

1 TR: 6.4 Listen and color. Then sing and point.

2 Look and circle ✔ or ✘.

VALUE **SAY NICE THINGS.**

1 ✔ ✘

2 ✔ ✘

3 ✔ ✘

1 TR: 6.5 Listen and say.

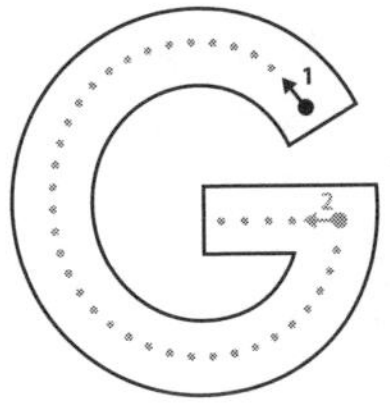

GORILLA

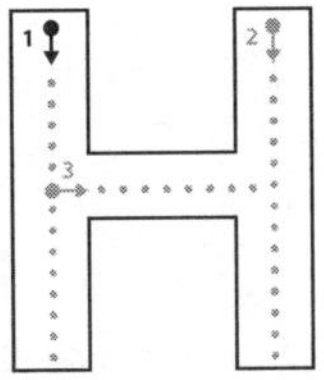

HIPPO

2 Trace.

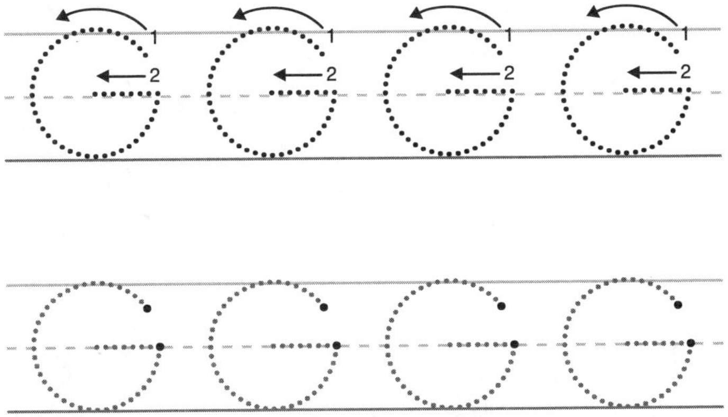

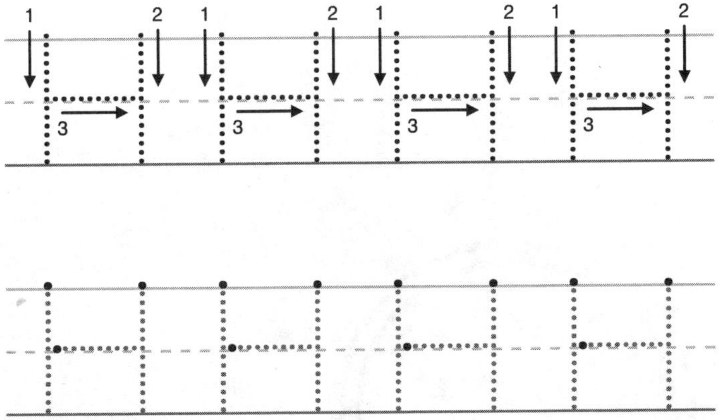

1 Look and match.

1 Draw, color, and say.

REVIEW: NEW WORDS: *ears, eyes, face, hair, mouth, nose; long, short*
STRUCTURE: *He has brown eyes. She has long hair.*

UNIT

7 MY THINGS

1 TR: 7.1 Listen and match.

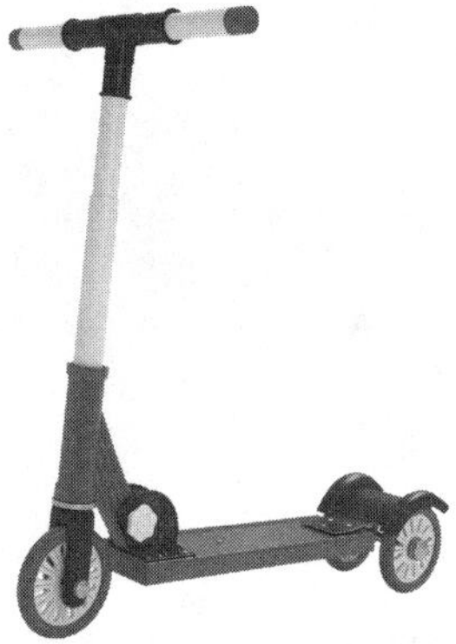

1 2 3 4 5 6 7

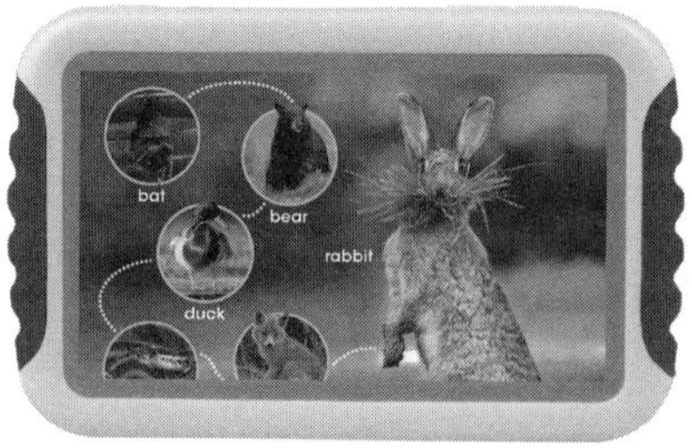

2 Point and say.

NEW WORDS: *bike, dinosaur, kite, puzzle, robot, scooter, tablet*

1 Draw one toy. Ask and answer.

1 TR: 7.2 Listen and circle. Then sing and point.

2 Look and circle ✔ or ✘.

VALUE **TAKE TURNS.**

1 ✔ ✘

2 ✔ ✘

3 ✔ ✘

1 TR: 7.3 Listen and say.

CAMEL

QUAIL

2 Trace.

1 Color and count.

1 Color. Ask and answer.

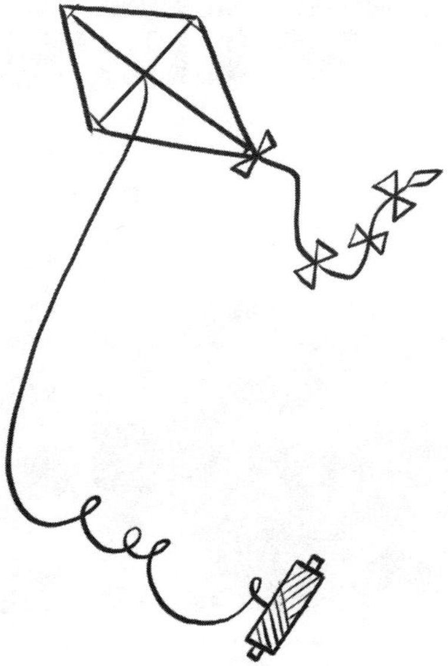

REVIEW: NEW WORDS: *bike, dinosaur, kite, puzzle, robot, scooter, tablet*
STRUCTURE: *Is this your kite? Yes, it is./No, it isn't.*

UNIT 8 BABIES

1 TR: 8.1 Listen and match.

2 TR: 8.2 Listen and point. Then say.

NEW WORDS: *baby, calf, chick, kitten, lamb, puppy; big, small*

1 TR: 8.3 Listen and point. Then say.

STRUCTURE: *There's one cow. There are two calves.*

1 TR: 8.4 Listen and point. Then color.

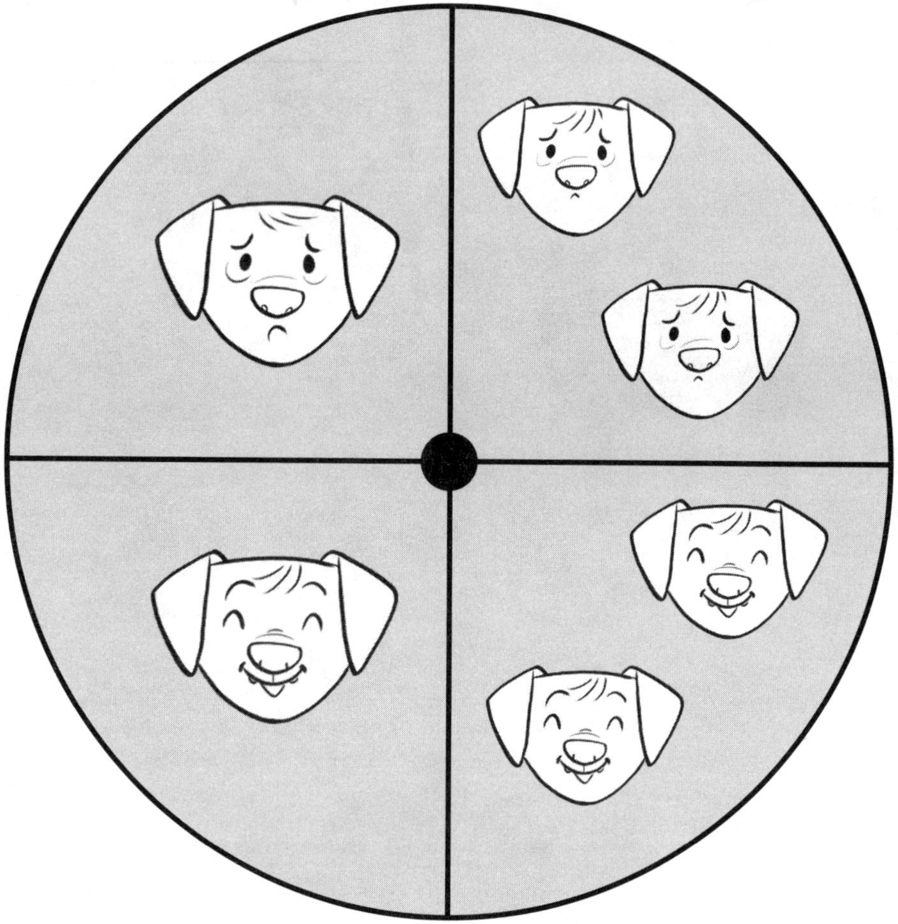

2 Look and circle ✔ or ✘.

VALUE **BE KIND.**

1 ✔ ✘

2 ✔ ✘

3 ✔ ✘

1 TR: 8.5 Listen and say.

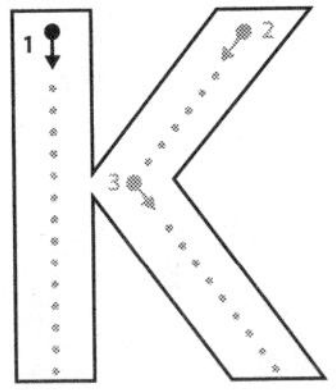

KANGAROO

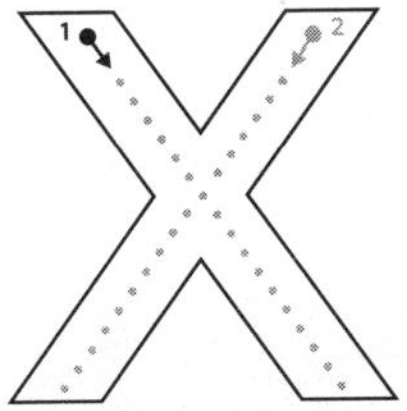

FO**X**

2 Trace.

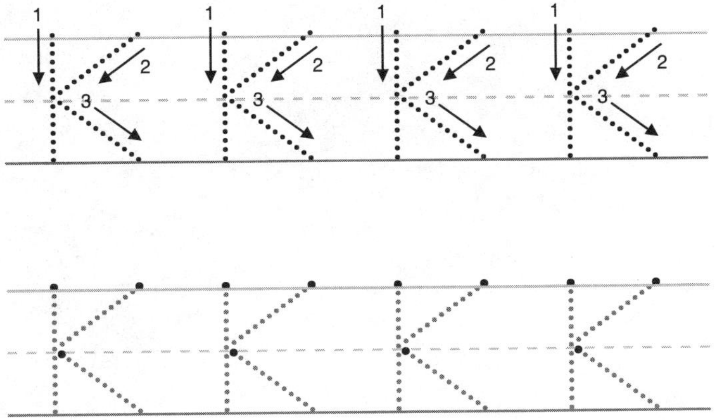

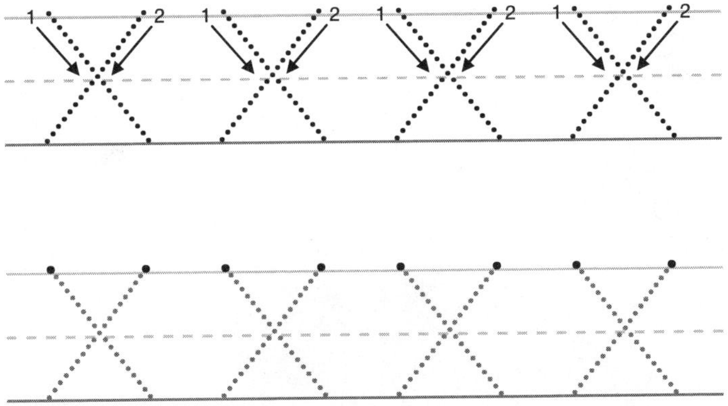

1 Match and say.

 VIDEO: SC: 16 *(optional)* **Content Words:** *ant, egg, ostrich*

1 Color and say.

REVIEW: NEW WORDS: *baby, calf, chick, kitten, lamb, puppy; big, small*
STRUCTURE: *There's one cow. There are two calves.*

UNIT

9 WHAT'S FOR DINNER?

1 TR: 9.1 Listen. Circle ✔ or ✘.

1 ✔ ✘

2 ✔ ✘

3 ✔ ✘

4 ✔ ✘

5 ✔ ✘

6 ✔ ✘

7 ✔ ✘

8 ✔ ✘

2 Point and say.

 NEW WORDS: *beans, bread, chicken, dinner, fish, noodles, rice, salad*

1 TR: 9.2 Listen and match. Then say.

1

2

3

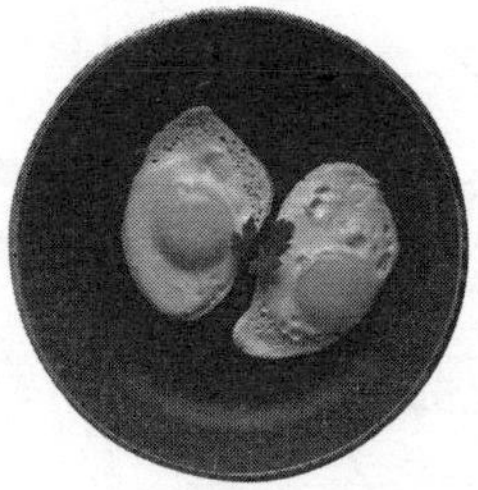

4

5

6

STRUCTURE: *What do you want? I want chicken, please.*

1 TR: 9.3 Listen and circle. Then color and sing.

2 Look and circle ✔ or ✘.

VALUE **HELP IN THE KITCHEN.**

1 ✔ ✘

2 ✔ ✘

3 ✔ ✘

1 TR: 9.4 Listen and say.

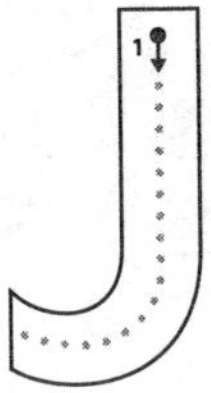

JAGUAR

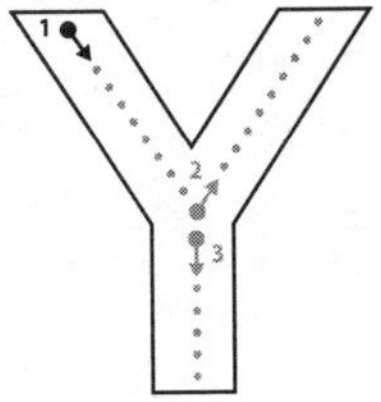

YAK

2 Trace.

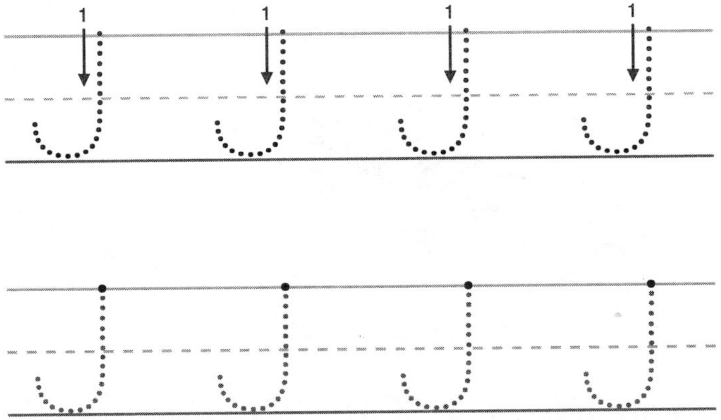

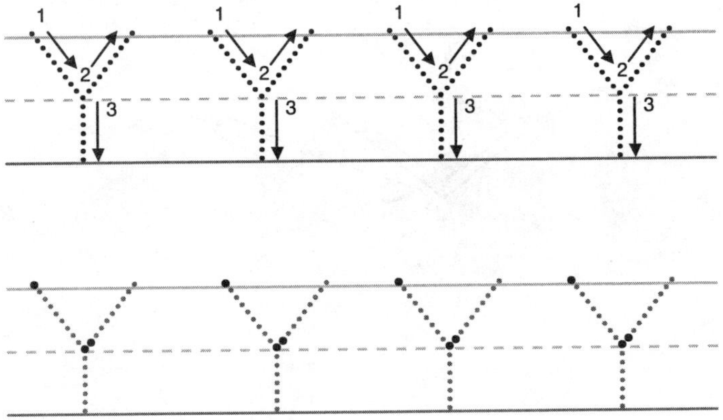

1 TR: 9.5 Let's make soup! Listen and circle.

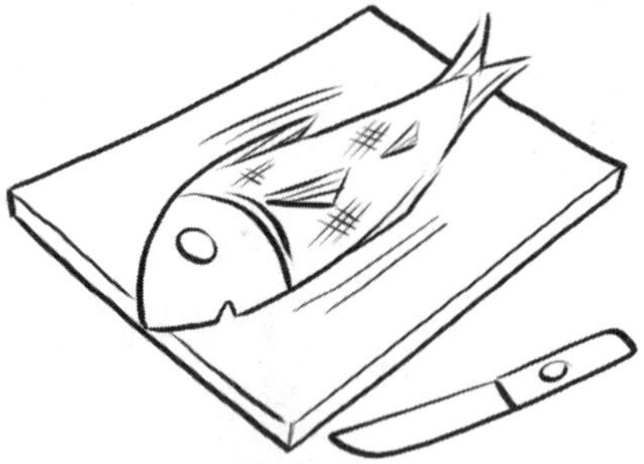

 VIDEO: SC: 18 *(optional)* **Content Words:** *cook, eat, onion, soup*

1 What's for dinner? Draw.

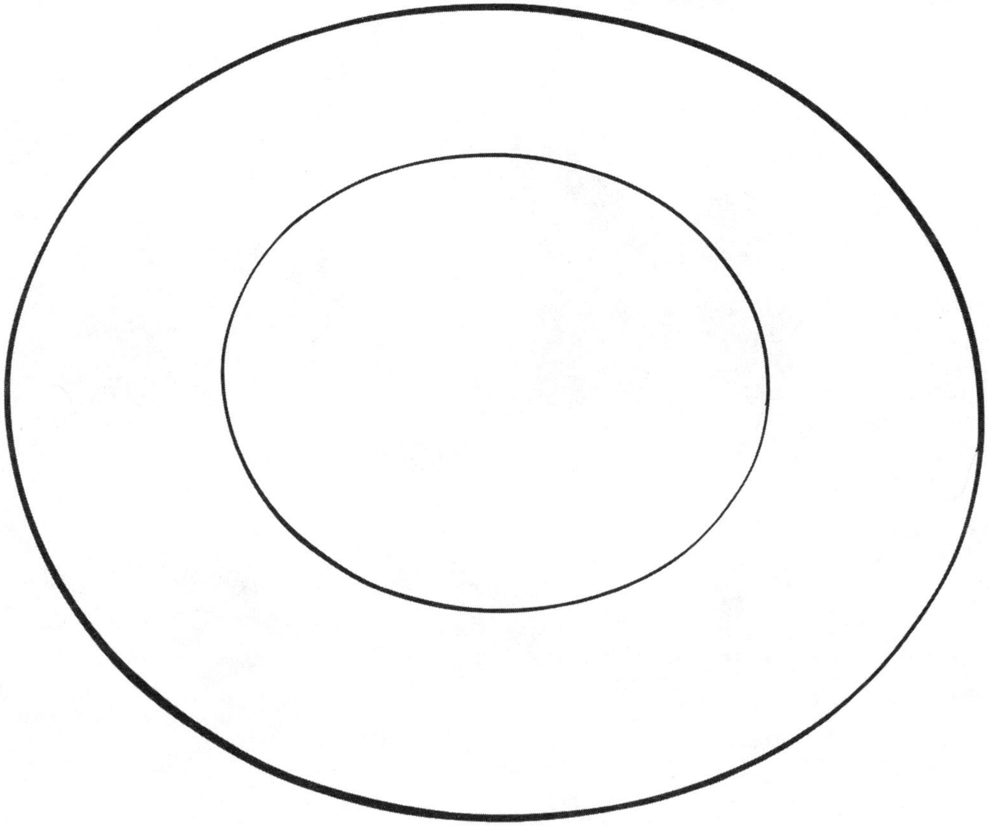

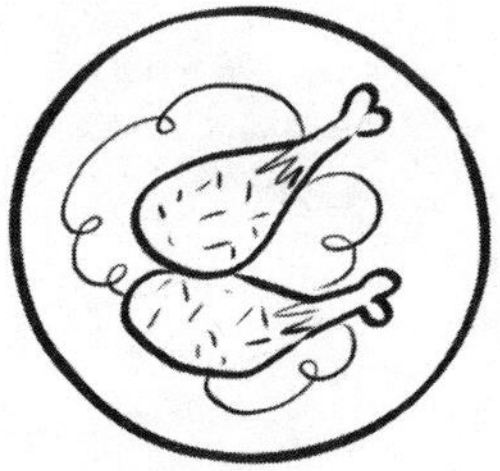

REVIEW: NEW WORDS: *beans, bread, chicken, dinner, fish, noodles, rice, salad*
STRUCTURE: *What do you want? I want chicken, please.*

UNIT 10 BUGS

1 TR: 10.1 Listen and match.

1 2 3 4 5 6 7

2 Look and say.

 NEW WORDS: *ant, bee, butterfly, caterpillar, ladybug, snail, spider*

1 TR: 10.2 Listen and match. Then point and say.

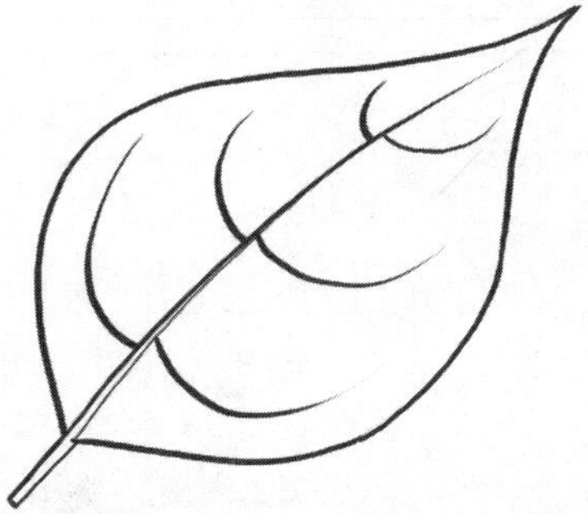

STRUCTURE: *Where's the caterpillar? It's on an apple.*

1 TR: 10.3 Listen and draw. Then sing and point.

2 Look and circle ✔ or ✗.

VALUE BE GOOD TO NATURE.

1 ✔ ✗

2 ✔ ✗

3 ✔ ✗

1 TR: 10.4 Listen and say.

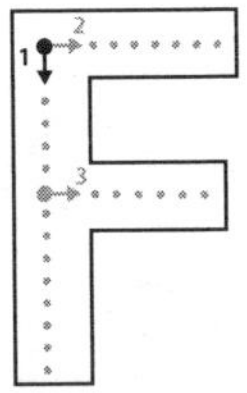

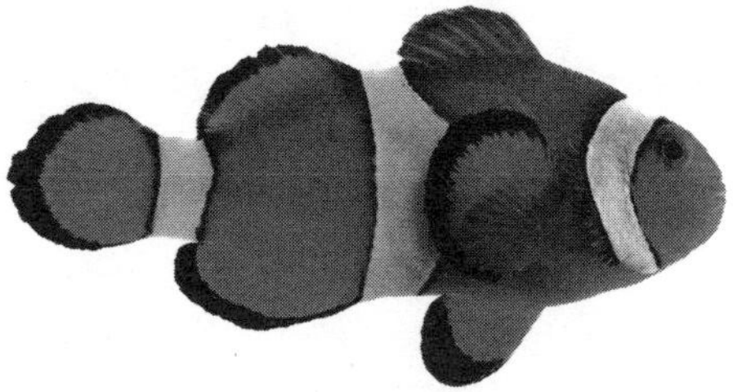

FISH

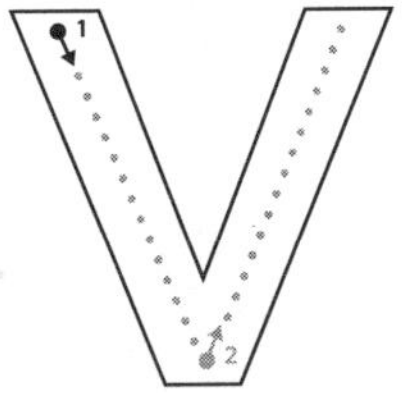

VULTURE

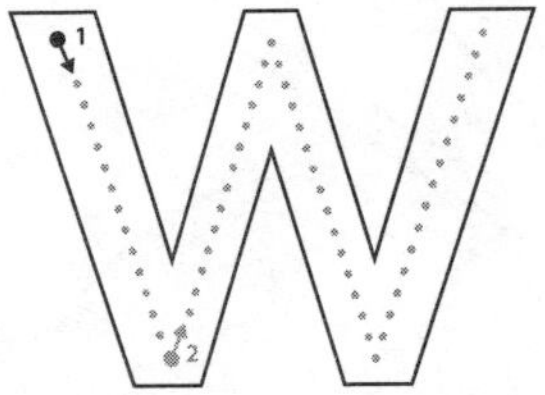

WOLF

2 Trace.

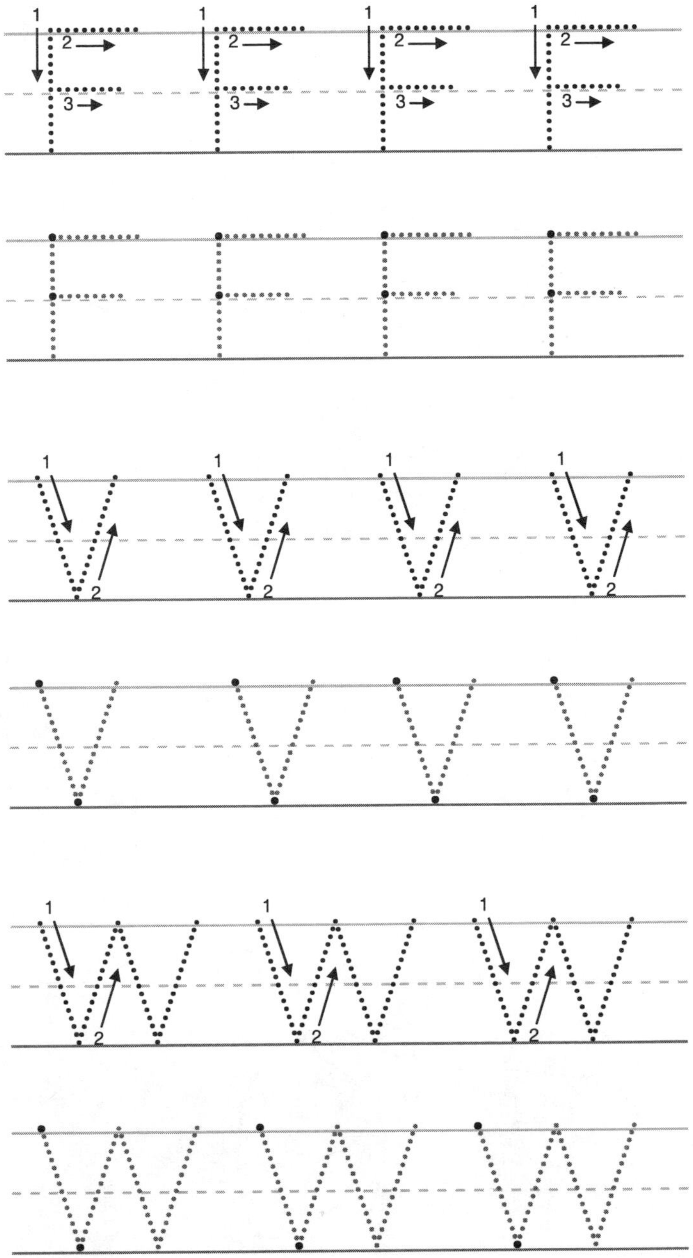

1 TR: 10.5 Listen and match. Color.

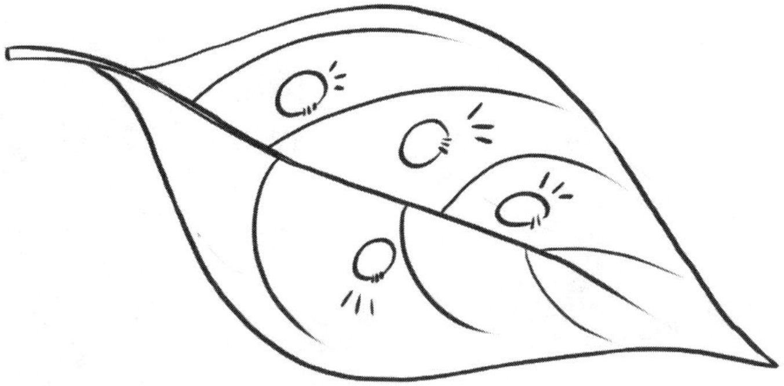

1 **2** **3** **4**

1 Look and say. Find. Then color.

REVIEW: NEW WORDS: *ant, bee, butterfly, caterpillar, ladybug, snail, spider*
STRUCTURE: *Where's the caterpillar? It's on an apple.*

CREDITS

PHOTOS: 2 (tl) Peter Dazeley/Photographer's Choice/Getty Images; (tm) Sergiy Tryapitsyn/Alamy Stock Photo; (tr) Joel Sartore/National Geographic Photo ARK/National Geographic Image Collection; (mtl) Chris Winsor/Moment/Getty Images; (mtm) Chayapon Bootboonneam/EyeEm/Getty Images; (mtr) Joel Sartore/National Geographic Image Collection; (ml) Super Prin/Shutterstock.com; (mm) Anna Kucherova/Shutterstock.com; (mr) Joel Sartore, National Geographic Photo ARK/National Geographic Image Collection; (bml) prochasson frederic/Shutterstock.com; (mbm) recebin/Shutterstock.com; (mbr) Joel Sartore/National Geographic Image Collection; (bl) Olhastock/Shutterstock.com; (bm) Mega Pixel/Shutterstock.com; (br) Joel Sartore/National Geographic Image Collection; **4** (tl) Mega Pixel/Shutterstock.com; (tml) nulinukas/Shutterstock.com; (tmr) Nenov Brothers Images/Shutterstock.com; (tr) Zhukov/Shutterstock.com; (bl) Fototocam/Shutterstock.com; (bm) © Annie Griffiths; (br) Arief Juwono/Moment/Getty Images; **7** (t) Joel Sartore, National Geographic Photo ARK/National Geographic Image Collection; (b) Joel Sartore/National Geographic Photo Ark/National Geographic Image Collection; **8** (tl) Sinead Hoben/Alamy Stock Photo; (tr) Ventura Carmona/Moment/Getty Images; (ml) Ullrich Gnoth/Alamy Stock Photo; (mr) TRphotos/Shutterstock.com; (bl) Imaginechina Limited/Alamy Stock Photo; (br) acilo/E+/Getty Images; **10** (tl) PhotoAlto/Belen Majdalani/PhotoAlto Agency RF Collections/Getty Images; (tml) Victoria Penafiel/Moment/Getty Images; (tmr) Aguru/E+/Getty Images; (tr) Wu Jibin Xinhua/eyevine/Redux; (bl) Tetyana Kaganska/Shutterstock.com; (bm) Laura Olivas/Moment/Getty Images; (br) ESB Professional/Shutterstock.com; **13** (t) Joel Sartore, National Geographic Photo ARK/National Geographic Image Collection; (b) Joel Sartore/National Geographic Image Collection; **16** (tl) Michael Nichols/National Geographic Image Collection; (tml) NaturesThumbPrint/iStock/Getty Images; (tmr) K Quinn Ferris/Shutterstock.com; (tr) Luka Hercigonja/Shutterstock.com; (bl) © Olivier Colle/Comedy Wildlife Photography Awards; (bm) Dave Montreuil/Shutterstock.com; (br) Menno Schaefer/Shutterstock.com; **19** (t) Joel Sartore, National Geographic Photo ARK/National Geographic Image Collection; (b) Joel Sartore, National Geographic Photo ARK/National Geographic Image Collection; **20** (tl) All-stock-photos/Shutterstock.com; (tm) Sergey Uryadnikov/Shutterstock.com; (tr) Daniel Rodriguez Garriga/Shutterstock.com; (bl) Coatesy/Shutterstock.com; (bm) Mitchell Krog/Gallo Images Roots RF collection/Getty Images; (br) Edwin Butter/Shutterstock.com; **22** (tl) Ruslan Kudrin/Shutterstock.com; (tml) Magdalena Wielobob/Shutterstock.com; (tmr) windu/Shutterstock.com; (tr) Tarzhanova/Shutterstock.com; (bl) adisa/iStock/Getty Images; (bm) NYS444/iStock/Getty Images; (br) Oxa/Shutterstock.com; **25** (t) Joel Sartore, National Geographic Photo ARK/National Geographic Image Collection; (b) Joel Sartore, National Geographic Photo ARK/National Geographic Image Collection; **28** (tl) RooM the Agency/Alamy Stock Photo; (tml) TheVisualsYouNeed/Shutterstock.com; (tmr) MoMorad/E+/Getty Images; (tr) Felix Mizioznikov/Shutterstock.com; (bl) David Patrick Valera/Moment/Getty Images; (bm) Elizabethsalleebauer/RooM/Getty Images; (br) © David Lazar; **31** (t) Joel Sartore, National Geographic Photo ARK/National Geographic Image Collection; (b) Joel Sartore, National Geographic Photo ARK/National Geographic Image Collection; **34** SanyaSM/E+/Getty Images; **37** (t) Joel Sartore, National Geographic Photo ARK/National Geographic Image Collection; (b) Joel Sartore, National Geographic Photo ARK/National Geographic Image Collection; **40** (tl) Besjunior/iStock/Getty Images; (tml) chengyuzheng/iStock/Getty Images; (tmr) CGinspiration/E+/Getty Images; (tr) Monthira/Shutterstock.com; (bl) Heidi Becker/Shutterstock.com; (bm) Hurst Photo/Shutterstock.com; (br) time4studio/Shutterstock.com; (br insert; tl) Dave Montreuil/Shutterstock.com; (br insert; tr) NaturesThumbPrint/iStock/Getty Images; (br insert; m) Luka Hercigonja/Shutterstock.com; (br insert; bl) K Quinn Ferris/Shutterstock.com; (br insert; br) Menno Schaefer/Shutterstock.com; (br insert; background) © Olivier Colle/Comedy Wildlife Photography Awards; **43** (t) Joel Sartore, National Geographic Photo ARK/National Geographic Image Collection; (b) Joel Sartore, National Geographic Photo ARK/National Geographic Image Collection; **46** (tl) Papilio/Alamy Stock Photo; (tml) Pete Ryan/National Geographic Image Collection; (tm) Claudia Nass/Alamy Stock Photo; (tmr) Design Pics Inc/National Geographic Image Collection; (tr) Vasilyev Alexandr/Shutterstock.com; (bl) Anatoliy Lukich/Shutterstock.com; (bml) Happy monkey/Shutterstock.com; (bm) mitsuaki-iwago/Minden Pictures; (bmr) Volodymyr Burdiak/Shutterstock.com; (br) Robert Garrigus/Alamy Stock Photo; **47** (tl) Tsekhmister/Shutterstock.com; (tm) photomaster/Shutterstock.com; (tr) Eric Isselee/Shutterstock.com; (mtl) Eric Isselee/Shutterstock.com; (mtr) Eric Isselee/Shutterstock.com; (mbl) Cherry-Merry/Shutterstock.com; (mbr) Kuttelvaserova Stuchelova/Shutterstock.com; (bl) Diane Kuhl/Shutterstock.com; (bm) MirasWonderland/Shutterstock.com; (br) Erik Lam/Shutterstock.com; **49** (t) Joel Sartore, National Geographic Photo ARK/National Geographic Image Collection; (b) Joel Sartore, National Geographic Photo ARK/National Geographic Image Collection; **50** (tl) phasinphoto/iStock/Getty Images; (tm) sruilk/Shutterstock.com; (tr) Wildlife GmbH/Alamy Stock Photo; (bl) Marc Pletcher/Shutterstock.com; (bm) Sergei25/Shutterstock.com; (bl) Aukid Phumsirichat/EyeEm/Getty Images; **52** (tl) jantima14/Shutterstock.com; (tml) Anfisa Kameneva/EyeEm/Getty Images; (tmr) Maria Uspenskaya/Shutterstock.com; (tr) Anna_Pustynnikova/Shutterstock.com; (bl) Eugene Mymrin/Moment/Getty Images; (bml) bigacis/Shutterstock.com; (bmr) Aleksandra Berzhets/Shutterstock.com; (br) Klaus Vedfelt/DigitalVision/Getty Images; **53** (tl) AS Food studio/Shutterstock.com; (tm) jantima14/Shutterstock.com; (tr) Tatiana Volgutova/Shutterstock.com; (ml) Yaruniv Studio/Shutterstock.com; (mm) goffkein.pro/Shutterstock.com; (mr) Timolina/Shutterstock.com; (bl) Aleksandra Berzhets/Shutterstock.com; (bm) BigBigbb1/Shutterstock.com; (br) Maks Narodenko/Shutterstock.com; **55** (t) Joel Sartore, National Geographic Photo ARK/National Geographic Image Collection; (b) Joel Sartore, National Geographic Photo ARK/National Geographic Image Collection; **58** (tl) khlungcenter/Shutterstock.com; (tml) Sailorr/Shutterstock.com; (tmr) guy42/Shutterstock.com; (tr) Aleksandar Grozdanovski/Shutterstock.com; (bl) Alik Mulikov/Shutterstock.com; (bm) Denis Tabler/Shutterstock.com; (br) Cameramannz/Shutterstock.com; **61** (t) Joel Sartore, National Geographic Photo ARK/National Geographic Image Collection; (m) Joel Sartore, National Geographic Photo ARK/National Geographic Image Collection; (b) Joel Sartore/National Geographic Image Collection; **Back Cover** Joel Sartore/National Geographic Image Collection.

ILLUSTRATIONS: 3, 53 Fabiana Faiallo; **6, 9, 11, 12, 14, 15, 17, 18, 21, 23, 24, 26, 27, 29, 30, 32, 33, 34, 35, 36, 38, 39, 41, 42, 44, 45, 48, 51, 54, 56, 57, 59, 60, 62, 63** Giovanni Giorgi Pierfranceschi.